The Transcending Divorce
Journal

Also by Alan Wolfelt

Healing A Child's Grieving Heart:
100 Practical Ideas for Families, Friends & Caregivers

Healing A Friend's Grieving Heart: 100 Practical Ideas
for Helping Someone You Love Through Loss

Healing A Teen's Grieving Heart: 100 Practical Ideas
for Families, Friends & Caregivers

Healing Your Grieving Heart: 100 Practical Ideas

The Journey Through Grief: Reflections on Healing

Living in the Shadow of the Ghosts of Grief:
Step Into the Light

Transcending Divorce: Ten Essential Touchstones
for Finding Hope and Healing Your Heart

The Transcending Divorce Support Group Guide:
Guidance and Meeting Plans for Facilitators

The Wilderness of Divorce: Finding Your Way

Companion
P R E S S

Companion Press is dedicated to the education and support
of both the bereaved and bereavement caregivers. We believe
that those who companion the bereaved by walking with them
as they journey in grief have a wondrous opportunity: to help
others embrace and grow through grief—and to lead fuller, more
deeply-lived lives themselves because of this important ministry.

For a complete catalog and ordering information, write or call:

Companion Press
The Center for Loss and Life Transition
3735 Broken Bow Road
Fort Collins, Colorado 80526
(970) 226-6050

www.centerforloss.com

The Transcending Divorce

Journal

Exploring the Ten Essential Touchstones

A companion workbook to
the book *Transcending Divorce*

Alan D. Wolfelt, Ph.D.

Companion
PRESS

Fort Collins, Colorado
An imprint of the Center for Loss and Life Transition

Companion Press is an imprint of the Center for Loss and Life Transition, 3735 Broken Bow Road, Fort Collins, Colorado 80526.

Printed in the United States of America.

17 16 15 14 13 12 11 10 09 08   5 4 3 2 1

ISBN: 978-1-879651-54-8

Contents

Introduction

"Writing is the most profound way of codifying your thoughts, the best way of learning from yourself who you are and what you believe."

Warren Bennis

I have written this journal as a companion to my book *Transcending Divorce: Ten Essential Touchstones for Finding Hope and Healing Your Heart.* My hope is that this guided journal can be a "safe place" for you to explore your experience with the ten essential Touchstones.

As you tell your story, your words will guide you on your unique journey through the wilderness of your divorce. I hope this resource will become your road map and guide you as you journal your way to what I'll define as integration of your divorce into your life.

The Value of Journaling

Journaling has proven to be an excellent way for many people to do the work of mourning when their marriage ends. Journaling is private and independent, yet it's still a great way to put things outside of yourself. I've been a counselor for a long time now (over 25 years!), and I've found that while it may not be for everyone, the process of putting the written word on paper is profoundly helpful to many people who experience a major life transition.

Journaling...

• helps you clarify your thoughts and feelings.

• creates a safe place of solace, a place where you can fully express yourself no matter what you are experiencing.

- clears out your naturally overwhelmed mind and full heart.

- helps you explore the pain you are experiencing and transforms it into something survivable.

- creates an opportunity to acknowledge the balance in your life between the sad and the happy.

- strengthens your awareness of how your divorce journey changes over time.

- maps out how you are changed and transformed by this experience.

- allows you to tap into the Touchstones of the book *Transcending Divorce*, the companion to this journal.

As one author observed, "When you write, you lay out a line of words. The line of words is a miner's pick, a woodcarver's gouge, a surgeon's probe. You wield it, and it digs a path you follow." To this I would add that a divorce journal can provide a lifeline when you are in the midst of the wilderness. As you learn, remember, and discover new things, you can and will integrate this divorce into your life and go on to find meaning and purpose in your future.

Journaling Suggestions

First, please remember that there is no "correct" or "right" way to use this journal. You will not be graded on how well you complete the pages that follow. Actually, I would suggest that you take your time. If you are using this resource as part of a support group experience, your leaders will probably encourage you to take your time as you complete this journal over several months.

If you are reading *Transcending Divorce* and completing this journal on your own, I suggest you find a trusted person who can be available to you if and when you want to talk out any thoughts and feelings the journal brings you. When I say trusted person, I mean someone who accepts you where you are right now in your divorce journey. This person shouldn't judge you or think it's his or her job to "get you over" your divorce quickly.

You will notice that in addition to the guided journal sections, in which you are asked to answer specific questions about your divorce experience, there are a number of "Free Write" pages. This is a dedicated space for you to freely write about whatever is on your heart as you are completing the journal. At the end of the journal, you will also find a section titled "Continuing Your Journey." This is a place to write down your ongoing thoughts and feelings about your divorce journey in the months to come.

• Setting

Choose a safe place to write in your journal. Naturally, journaling is usually easier to do in a quiet place that is free from interruptions and distractions.

• Privacy

This is your journal and yours alone. Remember—you don't have to share your journal or show it to anyone you don't want to. If you are participating in a support group, you may be invited to share some of what you write in your journal. Yet, keep in mind that sharing should always be optional, not mandatory.

• Honesty

In an effort to open yourself to your real experience, you must be honest with yourself. You must think your true thoughts, and write them out. You must feel your true feelings and express them.

Be Gentle With Yourself

Some people shy away from writing in a journal because they don't think they are good writers. It doesn't matter if you are a "good" writer or not, at least in the English teacher sense of that term. The point isn't to test your vocabulary or your punctuation or even your creative writing skills, but to explore what is on your mind and in your heart. Don't criticize what comes to paper. Ignore your penmanship and don't worry about grammar or spelling. Journaling is a breathing space on paper. Breathe deep and go forth!

Remember to Be Kind to Yourself

A journal is a confession. It simply listens as you write. Believe in your ability to set your intention to heal by using this journal as an instrument in your healing. Remember to be kind to yourself during this naturally difficult journey.

Sincerely,

Alan D. Wolfelt

Touchstone One

Open to the Presence of Your Loss

In the companion text....

We discussed the necessity of opening to the presence of the pain of your divorce experience. To heal in grief, you must honor—not avoid—the pain. One way to embrace the pain while at the same time maintaining hope for the future is by setting your intention to heal. Even as you "dose" your pain and set your intention to heal and transcend, remember that healing in grief does not happen quickly or efficiently. Also remember that the common perception of "doing well" in divorce grief is erroneous. To "do well" with your grief, you must not be strong and silent, but rather mourn all that you have lost openly and honestly.

As you were reading *Transcending Divorce*, you discovered that honoring your grief means "recognizing the value of" and "respecting" your grief. You learned that while it is not instinctive to view grief and the need to openly mourn as something to honor, the end of your marriage requires that you mourn. You also learned that to honor the grief surrounding your divorce is not self-destructive or harmful. It is self-sustaining and life-giving!

Describe the ways in which you have honored the grief that accompanies your divorce experience. If you feel you have not been honoring your divorce grief, write about ways you could begin to do so.

_____
_____
_____
_____
_____
_____
_____
_____
_____
_____
_____
_____
_____
_____
_____
_____
_____
_____
_____
_____
_____
_____
_____
_____
_____
_____
_____

Dosing Your Pain

You have learned that the pain of your divorce grief will keep trying to get your attention until you have the courage to gently, and in small doses, embrace it. How is the pain of your divorce grief trying to get your attention?

_____

_____

_____

_____

_____

_____

_____

_____

_____

Soul Work and Spirit Work

You have learned that there is an important distinction between "soul work" and "spirit work." In addition, you now realize that "soul work" precedes "spirit work" on the path to transcendence. Where do you see yourself right now in this process that you are now aware you must honor?

_____

_____

_____

_____

_____

_____

_____

_____

_____

Setting Your Intention to Heal and Transcend

When you set your intention to heal, you make a true commitment to positively influence the course of your divorce journey. You choose between being what I call a "passive witness" or an "active participant" in your divorce experience.

Describe below your understanding of the difference between being a "passive witness" to your experience or an "active participant."

_____

_____

_____

_____

_____

_____

_____

_____

_____

You learned that when you set your intention to heal and eventually transcend your divorce experience, you make a commitment to positively influence the course of your life. Use the space below to explore your intention or intentions to integrate this divorce into your life and ultimately heal and experience "integration."

_____

_____

_____

_____

_____

_____

_____

Integrating Your Divorce Grief

Integrating your divorce into your life does not happen quickly or efficiently. How do you feel about your capacity to go slow and be patient with yourself as you journey through this experience?

_____

_____

_____

_____

_____

_____

_____

_____

_____

_____

No Reward for Speed

Do you see yourself having the capacity to both "work at" and "surrender" to your grief surrounding your divorce? If so, why? If not, why not?

_____

_____

_____

_____

_____

_____

_____

_____

_____

_____

Face Any Inappropriate Expectations

Sometimes people around you give you messages that tell you to "be strong" in the face of your divorce. Has this happened to you? If so, write about it below.

_____

_____

_____

_____

_____

_____

_____

_____

_____

_____

Sometimes people who openly mourn the loss of their marriage feel ashamed of their thoughts, feelings, and behaviors. Do you feel any sense of shame or embarrassment about how you are mourning? If so, write about it below.

_____

_____

_____

_____

_____

_____

_____

_____

_____

_____

Staying Open to the Ripple Effects of Divorce

What ripple effects of loss apply to your unique experience?
Review this list and see which ones you identify with the most.
Write about the ones you have placed checkmarks beside. What
additional losses would you add to your list?

_____

_____

_____

_____

_____

_____

_____

_____

_____

_____

_____

_____

Divorce Grief is Not a Disease

While divorce grief is a powerful experience, so too is your
ability to help yourself heal. Write about any steps you've taken
(even baby steps) to help you begin to heal.

_____

_____

_____

_____

_____

_____

Free Write

_____

_____

_____

_____

_____

_____

_____

_____

_____

_____

_____

_____

_____

_____

_____

_____

_____

_____

_____

_____

_____

_____

_____

_____

_____

_____

_____

_____

_____

_____

Touchstone Two

Dispel the Misconceptions About Divorce and Grief

In the companion text....

We discovered that many of the perceptions we may have—and society often teaches us—about divorce and grief aren't true at all. For example, grieving and mourning your divorce are NOT the same thing. Getting a divorce does NOT mean you are a failure. Many misconceptions color our experience of divorce. The trick is to sort out fact from fiction. I hope this section of this journal will help you do just that!

Misconception 1: Grief and mourning are the same thing.

Did you believe that grieving the loss of your marriage and mourning the loss of your marriage were the same thing? If so, how has this misconception affected you?

_____

_____

_____

_____

_____

_____

_____

_____

_____

_____

_____

_____

_____

_____

_____

_____

_____

_____

_____

_____

_____

_____

_____

_____

Now that we've explored the difference between grief and mourning, in what ways do you see yourself *mourning* the loss of your marriage—that is, openly and honestly expressing your grief outside of yourself and in the presence of compassionate others?

_____

_____

_____

_____

_____

_____

_____

_____

_____

Do you see yourself having difficulty expressing your grief outside of yourself (mourning) in any ways? If so, what is difficult about this and why do you think this is the case? Note anything you might be able to do about expressing your grief outwardly.

_____

_____

_____

_____

_____

_____

_____

_____

_____

_____

_____

Misconception 2: If you get a divorce, you are a failure.

Have you ever heard someone say or imply, "If you get a divorce, you are a failure"? If so, how do you feel about that?

_____

_____

_____

_____

_____

_____

_____

_____

_____

_____

_____

Is there any part of you that feels like you are a failure because of your divorce? If so, how do you see that belief influencing you right now?

_____

_____

_____

_____

_____

_____

_____

_____

_____

_____

_____

_____

_____

What can you do to remind yourself that you are not a failure because you have experienced a divorce?

_____

_____

_____

_____

_____

_____

_____

_____

_____

_____

_____

Misconception 3: When you marry, you must stay committed to the thought that love is forever.

When you got married, did you think it would be forever? If so, where did this belief come from? What are your thoughts and feelings about this now?

_____

_____

_____

_____

_____

_____

_____

_____

_____

_____

_____

What are you doing to make sure you are not punishing yourself because your marriage didn't last forever?

_____
_____
_____
_____
_____
_____
_____
_____
_____
_____

Misconception 4: Divorce is a modern affliction.

Have you had the impression that divorce is a relatively recent phenomenon? Write about what it is like to acknowledge that divorce has been with us since marriage has been with us. How can you use this awareness to help you avoid feeling as if you are the only one to experience a divorce?

_____
_____
_____
_____
_____
_____
_____
_____
_____
_____
_____
_____

Misconception 5: If you get a divorce, you will never marry again.

Do you have any thoughts or fears that you may never again be in a committed love relationship? Write out your thoughts and feelings about this common misconception.

_____

_____

_____

_____

_____

_____

_____

_____

_____

_____

Misconception 6: The grief and mourning of divorce loss progress in predictable, orderly stages.

Have you heard about the "stages of grief"? If so, what is or was your opinion about this popular model of grief and loss?

_____

_____

_____

_____

_____

_____

_____

_____

_____

_____

The loss and grief that result from the divorce experience are sometimes a "one step forward, two steps backward" process. How could you help yourself during those inevitable times when you think you are moving backwards instead of forward?

_____

_____

_____

_____

_____

_____

_____

_____

_____

Misconception 7: You should try not to think or feel about the person you are divorcing or have divorced on holidays, anniversaries, or birthdays.

Since your divorce, have you encountered a holiday, anniversary date, or birthday? Describe the thoughts and feelings you have had on these days.

_____

_____

_____

_____

_____

_____

_____

_____

_____

_____

How have your friends and family responded to you on these special days? What has been helpful to you? What has not been helpful?

_____

_____

_____

_____

_____

_____

_____

_____

_____

What is the next upcoming holiday, anniversary, or birthday connected to your divorce? What expectations do you have about how you will feel and how you will cope during these days?

_____

_____

_____

_____

_____

_____

_____

_____

_____

Can you identify the people you can turn to for support, compassion and understanding during these naturally difficult times?

_____

_____

_____

_____

_____

_____

_____

_____

_____

_____

_____

Misconception 8: After you get a divorce, the goal should be to "get over it" and "move on" as quickly as possible.

Have you felt pressured to "get over" your divorce and "move on"? If so, how and why do you think this is the case?

_____

_____

_____

_____

_____

_____

_____

_____

_____

_____

_____

_____

Are you thinking or hoping that you should "get over" your divorce? If so, why? If not, why not?

_____

_____

_____

_____

_____

_____

_____

_____

_____

_____

_____

How do you (or could you) respond to friends, family, co-workers, etc. who encourage you, either outright or implicitly, to "move on" from your divorce?

_____

_____

_____

_____

_____

_____

_____

_____

_____

_____

_____

_____

_____

Have you found yourself crying at times in this process? If so, what have you done to help yourself understand that tears are a normal, even necessary, form of mourning your lost relationship?

_____

_____

_____

_____

_____

_____

_____

_____

_____

_____

_____

_____

_____

_____

How do you feel about the reality that you do not "get over" your divorce, but instead learn to integrate it into your life?

_____

_____

_____

_____

_____

_____

_____

_____

_____

_____

Misconception 9: Nobody can help you with your divorce transition.

Are you normally an independent person who does everything for yourself (and does not ask for help or support) or are you an interdependent person who relies on others for help with some things? Explain.

_____

_____

_____

_____

_____

_____

_____

_____

_____

_____

_____

Have you had anyone say things to you like, "You have to do this on your own." If so, what does this make you think and feel?

_____

_____

_____

_____

_____

_____

_____

_____

_____

_____

You will need to reach out to others to help you at this difficult time in your life. Do you believe this to be true? Why or why not?

_____

_____

_____

_____

_____

_____

_____

_____

_____

_____

_____

_____

List several people who are, or would be, naturally good support companions for you at this time. Also, are there any friends or family whom you realize cannot be supportive to you? If so, who are they and what are some of the reasons they are not able to be supportive to you ?

_____

_____

_____

_____

_____

_____

_____

_____

Misconception 10: When the grief and mourning of your divorce are integrated into your life, they will never come up again.

You have just read about how sometimes when you least suspect it, huge waves of grief, or "griefbursts," can come rolling in. Have you had any experiences with griefbursts you can write about?

_____

_____

_____

_____

_____

_____

_____

_____

_____

Do you have any "divorce-survivor role models" in your life—people who have openly mourned their lost marriages, and went on to rekindle meaning and purpose in their lives? If so, who are they? How do these people continue to acknowledge times when they have griefbursts?

_____

_____

_____

_____

_____

_____

_____

_____

_____

What do you do when you have griefbursts? Do you have people you can get support from when you experience these? If so, who are they, and what do you need from them during these naturally difficult times?

_____

_____

_____

_____

_____

_____

_____

_____

_____

_____

_____

_____

Additional Misconceptions About Divorce and Grief

Use the space below to write out any additional misconceptions you have experienced or observed and the ways in which you feel they have influenced your divorce journey.

_____

_____

_____

_____

_____

_____

_____

_____

_____

Free Write

_____

_____

_____

_____

_____

_____

_____

_____

_____

_____

_____

_____

_____

_____

_____

_____

_____

_____

_____

_____

_____

_____

_____

_____

_____

_____

_____

_____

_____

_____

_____

_____

Touchstone Three

Understanding the Uniqueness of Your Divorce Experience

In the companion text...

We developed an understanding that each person's divorce experience is unique. We also explored many influences that make your divorce wilderness experience unique to you and not exactly like anyone else's.

Influence #1: The circumstances of the divorce

Recognizing there are often aspects of divorce we do not ever totally "understand," describe what you believe are the circumstances of your divorce:

_____

_____

_____

_____

_____

_____

_____

_____

_____

_____

_____

_____

_____

_____

_____

_____

_____

_____

_____

_____

_____

_____

Did you see this divorce coming or was it sudden and unexpected? How did this affect you and the grief you are experiencing?

_____

_____

_____

_____

_____

_____

_____

_____

_____

_____

_____

Are there particular aspects of your divorce that have been difficult for you to openly acknowledge? If so, be gentle with yourself, but try to explore those aspects below. Remember —you don't have to share this information with anyone else unless you choose to do so.

_____

_____

_____

_____

_____

_____

_____

_____

_____

_____

_____

What other thoughts and feelings come to you as you reflect on the circumstances surrounding your divorce?

_____

_____

_____

_____

_____

_____

_____

_____

_____

_____

_____

Influence #2: Your Unique Personality

What are some adjectives you would use to describe yourself? What words would someone who knows you well use to describe you?

_____

_____

_____

_____

_____

_____

_____

_____

_____

_____

How do you think your unique personality is influencing your
unique divorce experience?

_____

_____

_____

_____

_____

_____

_____

_____

_____

_____

_____

_____

Do you think your personality has changed as a result of your
divorce? If so, how? If not, why not?

_____

_____

_____

_____

_____

_____

_____

_____

_____

_____

_____

How is your self-esteem right now?

_____

_____

_____

_____

_____

_____

_____

_____

_____

_____

_____

_____

_____

Do you think this divorce has impacted how you feel about yourself? If so, how?

_____

_____

_____

_____

_____

_____

_____

_____

_____

_____

_____

_____

_____

Influence #3: The People in Your Life

Do you have people in your life (family and friends) whom you can turn to for help and support? Who? Please list them below.

_____

_____

_____

_____

_____

What qualities do these people have that enable them to be supportive to you during this time in your life?

_____

_____

_____

_____

Are there people in your life you could turn to for support but for some reason you don't feel you can? If so, who and why?

_____

_____

_____

_____

Are you willing to accept support from family and friends? If not, why not?

_____

_____

_____

_____

_____

Sometimes well-meaning friends and family will hurt you unknowingly with their words. They may tell you:

- "I know just how you feel." (They don't)

- "You were never right for each other." (You may have felt you were at some point.)

- "Keep your chin up." (You have a right to be sad.)

- "Time heals all wounds." (Time helps, but it alone doesn't heal.)

- "There are more fish in the sea." (That may be, but your goal isn't to find a new "fish" right now.)

- "God wouldn't give you anything more than you can bear." (While faith may be of help to you, it is not helpful when people project a "you can take it" attitude anchored around God and faith.)

Have you had anyone say things like this to you? If so, write out an example and describe how it made you feel.

_____

_____

_____

_____

_____

_____

What are some things that people have said or done that have been helpful to you?

_____

_____

_____

_____

_____

_____

Do you have friends at work, at your place of worship, and/or at an organization you are part of who are supportive to you at this time? Who are these people and how can you continue to receive support from them?

_____

_____

_____

_____

_____

Are there some people you wish could be supportive to you but seem incapable of giving you what you need from them? If so, who are they and why do you think this is the situation?

_____

_____

_____

_____

Are you attending a support group as you work through this journal and companion text? If so, can you describe how this group experience is going for you so far?

_____

_____

_____

_____

_____

_____

_____

_____

_____

Are you seeing a counselor who is helping you work through this journal and companion text? If so, what has the counseling experience been like for you so far?

_____
_____
_____
_____
_____
_____
_____
_____
_____
_____
_____
_____

Influence #4: Your Children

How many children do you have? What are their names and ages?

_____
_____
_____
_____

How do you see each of your children responding to your divorce at this time?

_____
_____
_____
_____

What special needs do you see your children have since the divorce, and what have you done or can you do to help them with these needs? In what ways have you seen them grieve and mourn the losses they are experiencing related to the divorce?

_____

_____

_____

_____

How are you and your ex working together to ensure that your children remain well cared for during and after the divorce?

_____

_____

_____

_____

What resources (both human and written resources) can you turn to in an effort to help guide you in your efforts to help your children?

_____

_____

_____

_____

What questions or concerns do you have regarding your children?

_____

_____

_____

_____

Who can you turn to in an effort to explore the questions or concerns you have noted above?

_____

_____

_____

_____

_____

_____

_____

_____

_____

_____

_____

_____

Influence #5: Your Gender

Do you think that being a man or woman affects how you are experiencing your divorce grief? If so, how? If not, why not?

_____

_____

_____

_____

Has your gender influenced how people support or don't support you in your divorce transition? If so, how?

_____

_____

_____

_____

During this experience, do you see any advantages to being a man (if you are a man) who is going through divorce or to being a woman (if you are a woman) going through divorce?

_____

_____

_____

_____

_____

Influence #6: Your Cultural/Ethnic Background

What is your cultural/ethnic background?

_____

_____

_____

_____

How do you see this background influencing your divorce experience?

_____

_____

_____

_____

If you were asked to express them, what would you say some of the family "rules" were about marriage and divorce when you were growing up? What are some of the family rules that exist for you right now? In what ways, if any, do you see these rules affecting you right now?

_____

_____

_____

_____

How do you feel about these rules and their helpfulness or unhelpfulness to you as you encounter your divorce experience?

_____

_____

_____

_____

_____

Influence #7: Your Religious or Spiritual Background

Did you grow up with certain religious or spiritual teachings? Take a moment to describe them here.

_____

_____

_____

_____

_____

What, if anything, did you learn about marriage and divorce from these teachings noted above?

_____

_____

_____

_____

_____

Have your religious or spiritual teachings changed over time? If so, describe how they have changed.

_____

_____

_____

_____

_____

How has this divorce affected your belief system?

_____

_____

_____

_____

_____

Has anyone around you stated that it is a "sin" to get a divorce?
If so, describe this experience and your thoughts and feelings
about it.

_____

_____

_____

_____

_____

_____

Do you have people around you who understand and support you
in your belief system? If so, who are these people and how can
they help you now?

_____

_____

_____

_____

Do you think your faith, religion, or spiritual background is
playing a part in your healing process? Please explain.

_____

_____

_____

_____

Influence #8: Other Changes, Crises, or Stresses in Your Life Right Now

What other changes, crises, or stresses have come about in your life either as a result of the divorce or coincidentally during this same time?

_____

_____

_____

_____

_____

How do you see these other changes, crises, or stresses influencing your life right now?

_____

_____

_____

_____

_____

How are they affecting your need to mourn your divorce loss?

_____

_____

_____

_____

_____

Who can you turn to right now to help you cope with these additional changes, crises or stresses?

_____

_____

_____

_____

Infuence #9: Your Physical Health

You will be writing more about this on page 96 of this journal. For now, take a moment to write about how you are feeling physically right now.

_____

_____

_____

_____

_____

_____

_____

_____

_____

_____

What are you doing to take care of your body right now?

_____

_____

_____

_____

_____

_____

_____

_____

_____

_____

_____

_____

_____

Influence #10: Your Financial Health

How would you describe your current financial situation?

_____

_____

_____

_____

_____

Have your finances changed as a result of your divorce? If so, how?

_____

_____

_____

_____

_____

Has your work life changed as a result of the divorce? If so, how?

_____

_____

_____

_____

_____

Have you sought some help to assess your financial health? If not, what can you do about this? If so, what have you done and what have you learned you need to be doing related to your finances?

_____

_____

_____

_____

Other Factors Influencing Your Divorce Journey

Are there other factors, large or small, that are influencing your divorce experience right now? If so, write about them below.

_____

_____

_____

_____

_____

_____

_____

_____

_____

_____

_____

_____

_____

_____

_____

_____

_____

_____

_____

_____

_____

_____

_____

_____

_____

_____

_____

_____

Free Write

_____

_____

_____

_____

_____

_____

_____

_____

_____

_____

_____

_____

_____

_____

_____

_____

_____

_____

_____

_____

_____

_____

_____

_____

_____

_____

_____

_____

_____

_____

Touchstone Four

Explore Your Feelings of Loss

In the companion text...

We noted that it is vitally important to experience and express the multitude of feelings that are part of your divorce journey. We emphasized that whatever your thoughts and feelings are, they are normal and necessary. Feelings aren't right or wrong. They just are. Naming the feelings and acknowledging them are the first steps to integrating them into your life. It's actually the process of becoming friendly with your feelings that will help you eventually heal and become whole again.

Before exploring some of the potential responses to your divorce experience, please take a few minutes and describe how you are feeling right now. In the space below, complete the following statement:

Right now I'm feeling....

_____

_____

_____

_____

_____

_____

_____

_____

_____

_____

Shock, Numbness Denial, Disbelief

Have feelings of shock and numbness been a part of your divorce journey? Can you describe what that has been like for you?

_____

_____

_____

_____

_____

_____

_____

_____

_____

_____

Do you feel that your shock and numbness helped you survive during the early parts of your experience? If yes, how? If not, why not?

_____

_____

_____

_____

_____

_____

_____

_____

_____

_____

_____

How has your divorce brought on feelings of shock, numbness, denial and disbelief?

_____

_____

_____

_____

_____

_____

_____

_____

_____

_____

_____

Do you feel you are or have been in denial about your divorce? Please explain.

_____

_____

_____

_____

_____

_____

_____

_____

_____

_____

_____

Are you learning to allow yourself to acknowledge the divorce in small doses in between periods of denial? In the companion book, I called this "evading and encountering." If you are stuck on evading, how can you help yourself encounter the reality of the divorce?

_____

_____

_____

_____

_____

_____

_____

_____

_____

How have your feelings of shock, numbness, denial and disbelief changed over time? If they have not changed over time, what do you think accounts for that?

_____

_____

_____

_____

_____

_____

_____

_____

_____

_____

_____

_____

Disorganization/Confusion

Have you experienced any disorganization and confusion as part of your divorce experience? If so, describe what this has been like for you.

_____

_____

_____

_____

_____

_____

_____

_____

_____

Have you experienced any restlessness, agitation or impatience during your divorce wilderness journey? If so, describe what this has been like for you.

_____

_____

_____

_____

_____

_____

_____

_____

_____

_____

_____

Do you keep starting tasks but have trouble finishing them? Do you forget what you are saying mid-sentence? Are you having trouble getting through your day-to-day commitments? Name some of the ways your disorganization and confusion are affecting your life.

_____

_____

_____

_____

_____

_____

_____

_____

_____

_____

What are you doing to express your feelings of disorganization and confusion?

_____

_____

_____

_____

_____

_____

_____

_____

_____

_____

_____

_____

Anxiety, Panic, Fear

Have you felt any feelings of anxiety, panic, and fear as part of your divorce journey? If so, please explain.

_____

_____

_____

_____

_____

_____

_____

_____

_____

_____

What are you most anxious or afraid of right now?

_____

_____

_____

_____

_____

_____

_____

_____

_____

_____

_____

What have you been doing to help yourself with your feelings of anxiety, panic and fear?

_____

_____

_____

_____

_____

_____

_____

_____

_____

_____

_____

_____

_____

Explosive Emotions

Have you felt any anger, hate, blame, terror, resentment, rage, jealousy, vindictiveness, and/or bitterness surrounding your divorce experience? If so, which of these feelings have you experienced? If not, write out why you think these feelings have not been a part of your experience. Several potential protest emotions are listed below, with space for you to write about each of them.

Anger

_____

_____

_____

_____

_____

_____

Hate

_____

_____

_____

_____

_____

_____

Blame

_____

_____

_____

_____

_____

Terror

_____

_____

_____

_____

_____

_____

Resentment

_____

_____

_____

_____

_____

_____

Rage

_____

_____

_____

_____

_____

_____

Jealousy

_____

_____

_____

_____

_____

_____

Vindictiveness

_____
_____
_____
_____
_____
_____

Bitterness

_____
_____
_____
_____
_____

Have people around you been upset by your expression of any of these explosive emotions? Explain.

_____
_____
_____
_____
_____

What are you doing to express your explosive emotions in healthy ways?

_____
_____
_____
_____

Are you seeing some perturbation (movement) in how you experience your explosive emotions? Or, by contrast, do you feel "stuck" in your explosive emotions? What can you do to help yourself with your explosive emotions?

_____

_____

_____

_____

_____

_____

_____

_____

_____

_____

Guilt, Regret, Self-blame, Shame, Rejection, Worthlessness, Failure

Have you had any "if onlys" as part of your experience? If so, write about your if-onlys. How are you expressing and coping with them at this point in the journey?

_____

_____

_____

_____

_____

_____

_____

_____

_____

_____

_____

In the companion book, I made a distinction between "real" guilt and "false" guilt. Describe below how either one of these might apply to you during your divorce transition.

_____

_____

_____

_____

_____

_____

_____

_____

_____

_____

Do you have any of the following sub-types of guilt?

Relief-guilt   Longstanding personality-guilt   Joy-guilt

I invite you to write about any of the above that apply to you.

_____

_____

_____

_____

_____

_____

_____

_____

_____

_____

_____

Are you experiencing any of the following feelings as part of your experience?

Self-blame   Shame   Rejection   Worthlessness   Failure

I invite you to circle those above that apply to you, if any, and write about them below.

_____

_____

_____

_____

_____

_____

_____

_____

_____

What are you doing to increase or bolster your self-esteem?

_____

_____

_____

_____

_____

_____

_____

_____

_____

_____

_____

_____

_____

What are you doing to give expression to and get support for any of the feelings in this section that have application to your divorce experience?

_____

_____

_____

_____

_____

_____

_____

_____

_____

_____

_____

_____

Sadness, Depression, Loneliness, Vulnerability

Have you felt any sadness, depression, loneliness and vulnerability during your divorce experience? If so, which of these feelings have been, or currently are, a part of your life right now? If not, write about why you think these feelings have not been a part of your divorce.

Sadness

_____

_____

_____

_____

_____

_____

Depression

_____

_____

_____

_____

Loneliness

_____

_____

_____

_____

Vulnerability

_____

_____

_____

_____

Are there certain days or times when you have felt these feelings more than others?

_____

_____

_____

_____

_____

What additional reflections do you have about feelings of loneliness and vulnerability?

_____

_____

_____

_____

When you feel sad, what can you do to help yourself embrace your sadness instead of move away from it?

_____

_____

_____

_____

What specific triggers make you feel sad at this time?

_____

_____

_____

_____

Have you had any thoughts of suicide during your divorce transition?

_____

_____

_____

_____

Keep in mind that transient, passive thoughts of suicide during times of grief and loss are not uncommon, but persistent, active thoughts of suicide are not normal. If you are actively considering or making plans to take your own life, put down this journal this very moment and call someone who will help you get the support you need. If this is an emergency, call 911 immediately.

What are you doing to express your sadness and depression?

_____

_____

_____

_____

Do you think you might be clinically depressed? If yes, review the chart on page 93 in the companion book and determine if you meet any of the criteria for clinical depression. Do you exhibit any of the listed characteristics of clinical depression? If yes, write down your physician's name and phone number in the space below then put down this journal, go to the phone, and make an appointment to see him or her as soon as possible. Remember that getting help for your depression does not mean you are weak, it means you are strong.

Physician's name_____ Phone_____

Relief, Release, Happiness, Euphoria, Hope

Have you felt any relief, release, happiness, euphoria and hope surrounding your divorce experience? If so, which of these feelings are part of your life right now? If not, write out why you think these feelings have not been a part of your divorce.

Relief

_____

_____

_____

_____

Release

_____

_____

_____

_____

Happiness

_____

_____

_____

Euphoria

_____

_____

_____

_____

Hope

_____

_____

_____

_____

Have you been expressing any of these feelings? How? If not, why not?

_____

_____

_____

_____

When you have expressed these feelings, how have people around you responded?

_____

_____

_____

_____

What do you plan to do to continue to express these feelings?

_____

_____

_____

_____

_____

Are you having any other feelings that haven't been covered in this section of the journal? Please take a few minutes to explain them here.

_____

_____

_____

_____

_____

_____

_____

_____

Free Write

_____

_____

_____

_____

_____

_____

_____

_____

_____

_____

_____

_____

_____

_____

Touchstone Five

Recognize You Are Not Crazy

In the companion text...

We discussed that it is common for people who are divorcing to feel that they are going crazy. Many of the thoughts and feelings you will experience in your journey through divorce are so different from your everyday reality that you may feel like you're going crazy. You're not. You are grieving and mourning a major life transition. This chapter explores a number of potential thoughts, feelings and behaviors that contribute to your feeling this way.

Sudden Changes in Mood

Have you experienced some rollercoaster mood changes during this divorce experience? Please explain.

_____

_____

_____

_____

_____

_____

_____

_____

_____

_____

Leftover or Residual Attachment

Have you experienced some feelings of lingering attachment to your former life partner? If so, what has this been like for you and what have you done with these feelings?

_____

_____

_____

_____

_____

_____

_____

_____

_____

_____

_____

Rethinking and Retelling the Story

Are you rethinking and/or retelling the story of your marriage and divorce over and over again? If so, what are you noticing that you are focusing on as you think and/or talk about your marriage and divorce? Take some time to describe it here.

_____

_____

_____

_____

_____

_____

_____

_____

_____

Time Distortion

Has time seemed distorted to you as part of your divorce experience? Take a moment to describe this experience here.

_____

_____

_____

_____

_____

_____

_____

_____

_____

_____

Self-Focus

Have you felt the need to focus on yourself and pay less attention to others in your divorce experience? Write about your thoughts here.

_____

_____

_____

_____

_____

_____

_____

_____

_____

_____

_____

_____

Powerlessness and Helplessness

Has your divorce experience made you feel powerless or helpless at times? In what ways?

_____

_____

_____

_____

_____

_____

_____

_____

_____

_____

Griefbursts and Triggers

Have you had any griefbursts as part of your divorce journey?
If yes, give an example or two of where you were and what
happened.

_____

_____

_____

_____

_____

_____

_____

_____

_____

Crying and Sobbing

Do you find yourself expressing your feelings by crying or
sobbing? If so, how do you feel after you are done crying or
sobbing? If you are not crying at all, why do you think that is?

_____

_____

_____

_____

_____

_____

_____

_____

Borrowed Tears

Have you had any experience with borrowed tears? If so,
describe when this has happened and what it was like for you.

_____

_____

_____

_____

_____

_____

_____

_____

_____

_____

_____

_____

Painful Linking Objects and Memorabilia

Do you have some linking objects or memorabilia connected
to your relationship? If so, what do you have? What have you
done—or what do you plan to do—with these items?

_____

_____

_____

_____

_____

_____

_____

_____

_____

Carried Grief

Do you have any awareness that you might have some carried grief from prior losses? If so, explain. Also, what might you be able to do to give some attention to these prior losses?

_____

_____

_____

_____

_____

_____

_____

_____

_____

_____

Suicidal Thoughts

Have you contemplated suicide at any time before or after your divorce? If yes, write more about your thoughts here. Also, see page 67 of this journal for more on suicidal thoughts and determining if you may need additional help.

_____

_____

_____

_____

_____

_____

_____

Medicating Your Feelings with Drugs and Alcohol

Have you been using alcohol or drugs to dull or push away your pain related to your divorce experience? If so, describe what your alcohol or drug habits have been. Also, explore what you could do to help yourself related to this important area.

_____

_____

_____

_____

_____

_____

_____

_____

_____

_____

_____

Have you used any of the other behaviors described in this section (e.g., excess eating, premature replacement of the relationship, excess busyness, etc.) to numb your sorrow? If so, describe these behaviors below.

_____

_____

_____

_____

_____

_____

_____

_____

_____

_____

_____

Do you have a tendency to have an addictive personality? If so, describe how that may be influencing some of your behavior right now.

_____

_____

_____

_____

_____

_____

_____

_____

_____

_____

_____

_____

Dreams and Nightmares

Have you been having any dreams about your marriage, your divorce or your ex-spouse? If so, describe them here.

_____

_____

_____

_____

_____

_____

_____

_____

Have you been having any disturbing nightmares about your divorce or ex-spouse? If so, describe them here.

_____

_____

_____

_____

_____

_____

_____

_____

_____

_____

_____

_____

_____

Anniversaries and Holiday Occasions

In general, what have your birthday, anniversary and holiday occasions been like since your divorce? Write about your experiences below.

_____

_____

_____

_____

_____

_____

_____

_____

_____

_____

_____

Free Write

_____
_____
_____
_____
_____
_____
_____
_____
_____
_____
_____
_____
_____
_____
_____
_____
_____
_____
_____
_____
_____
_____
_____
_____
_____
_____
_____
_____
_____
_____
_____

Touchstone Six

Understand the Six Needs of Divorce Transition

In the companion text...

We introduced the six needs of divorce transition. Remember, the six needs are not orderly or predictable. You will probably jump around in random fashion while working on them. You will address each need as you are ready to do so. Your awareness of these needs, however, will give you a participative, action-oriented approach to integrating this transition into your life as opposed to a perception of this life transition as something you passively experience.

Need 1: Acknowledge the Reality of the Divorce

How do you see yourself in acknowledging the reality of your divorce?

_____

_____

_____

_____

_____

Do you think time is playing a part in where you are with this need? If so, how?

_____

_____

_____

_____

_____

Do you find yourself replaying events surrounding the divorce? If so, how do you think this replay might help you acknowledge the reality of the divorce?

_____

_____

_____

_____

_____

What can you do to continue to work on this need?

_____

_____

_____

_____

_____

Need 2: Let Yourself Feel the Pain of the Loss

Are you able to allow yourself to express the pain of the divorce? In what ways are you expressing your pain?

_____

_____

_____

_____

_____

_____

_____

_____

_____

Do you think that time is playing a part in where you are with this need?

_____

_____

_____

_____

_____

_____

To whom have you expressed your feelings of pain?

_____

_____

_____

_____

_____

_____

Write about what expressing your feelings has been like for you.

_____

_____

_____

_____

_____

_____

_____

_____

_____

_____

What can you do to continue to work on this need?

_____

_____

_____

_____

_____

_____

_____

Need 3: Shift Your Relationship With Your Former Spouse

Do you see your relationship with your former spouse shifting? How are you working on shifting this relationship?

_____

_____

_____

_____

_____

What kind of things have you done to restructure and redefine your relationship?

_____

_____

_____

_____

_____

_____

_____

What can you do to continue to work on this need?

_____

_____

_____

_____

_____

_____

_____

Need 4: Develop a New Self-Identity

Where do you see yourself in developing a new self-identity?

_____

_____

_____

_____

_____

_____

_____

What identity changes have you experienced as a result of your divorce?

_____

_____

_____

_____

_____

_____

_____

_____

How do you see people treating you differently as a result of your changed identity?

_____

_____

_____

_____

_____

_____

_____

_____

What, if any, positive changes in your self-identity have you noticed since the divorce?

_____

_____

_____

_____

_____

_____

What can you do to continue to work on this need?

_____

_____

_____

_____

_____

_____

_____

Need 5: Search for Meaning

Where do you see yourself in your search for meaning?

_____

_____

_____

_____

_____

_____

Do you find yourself revisiting your "story" or account of the marriage and divorce as you go backward on your path to go forward? If so, describe some of this experience.

_____

_____

_____

_____

_____

_____

_____

Have you found yourself exploring any faith or spiritual
questions as part of your search for meaning? If so, describe
them here.

_____

_____

_____

_____

_____

_____

_____

Have you started to work on some short-term and long-term
goals that will help you have meaning and purpose in your future
life? If so, describe them below.

_____

_____

_____

_____

_____

_____

_____

What can you do to continue to work on this need?

_____

_____

_____

_____

_____

_____

_____

Need 6: Let Others Help You—Now and Always

Where do you see yourself in letting supportive people help you—now and always?

_____

_____

_____

_____

_____

_____

_____

Who do you turn to for help?

_____

_____

_____

_____

_____

_____

What do these people do or say that lets you know they are there to support you?

_____

_____

_____

_____

_____

_____

_____

Are you getting support from others who have experienced a divorce? If so, what is that like for you?

_____
_____
_____
_____
_____
_____
_____
_____
_____
_____
_____

What can you do to continue to work on this need?

_____
_____
_____
_____
_____
_____
_____
_____
_____
_____
_____
_____
_____

Free Write

_____

_____

_____

_____

_____

_____

_____

_____

_____

_____

_____

_____

_____

_____

_____

_____

_____

_____

_____

_____

_____

_____

_____

_____

_____

_____

_____

Touchstone Seven

Nurture Yourself

In the companion text...

We reminded ourselves of the need to be self-nurturing in grief. Remember—you have special needs as you journey through the wilderness of divorce, and one of the most important needs right now is to be compassionate with yourself. This Touchstone is a gentle reminder to be kind and gentle to yourself as you journey through the wilderness of your divorce. We then explored the five realms in which it is critical to nurture yourself:

• Physical

• Emotional

• Cognitive

• Social

• Spiritual

Nurturing Yourself: The Physical Realm

Is your body letting you know that it feels distressed right now? If so, how?

_____

_____

_____

_____

_____

_____

_____

How are you sleeping?

_____

_____

_____

_____

_____

_____

How are you eating?

_____

_____

_____

_____

_____

_____

_____

Of the Guidelines for Good Health (pp. 136-140), which do you feel you are following right now? List them here.

_____

_____

_____

_____

_____

_____

_____

_____

_____

_____

_____

Nurturing Yourself: The Emotional Realm

What have you been doing to acknowledge and express your feelings?

_____

_____

_____

_____

_____

_____

_____

_____

_____

_____

Draw a "Divorce Grief Map" below. Make a circle on the center of the page and label it "my divorce." This circle represents your thoughts and feelings connected to your divorce. Now draw a line out of this circle and label each line with a feeling that has been, or currently is, a part of your experience. If you don't have room on this page to make your grief map, get a big piece of paper and do it there. Remember—you will not be graded for your artistic abilities. Just do it!

Have you been journaling, either in this journal or in a different journal? If so, write about what that has been like for you.

_____

_____

_____

_____

_____

_____

_____

What kinds of music touch your heart and soul? List your favorite artists and types of music here. How does music help you in terms of accessing your feelings?

_____

_____

_____

_____

_____

_____

Make a list of everyday activities that give you pleasure. Pick something from this list each day and do it.

_____

_____

_____

_____

_____

_____

_____

Affirmation: Write down everything you like about yourself. (I gave you one entire page because I want a long list!)

_____
_____
_____
_____
_____
_____
_____
_____
_____
_____
_____
_____
_____
_____
_____
_____
_____
_____
_____
_____
_____
_____
_____
_____

Have you been experiencing "skin hunger"? If yes, describe how it makes you feel.

_____

_____

_____

_____

_____

_____

_____

Nurturing Yourself: The Cognitive Realm

Have your short-term memory and ability to concentrate been affected by your divorce? If so, how?

_____

_____

_____

_____

_____

_____

Are you making an effort to not make too many changes too quickly right now? Are there some big decisions you have simply had to make? Write about this below.

_____

_____

_____

_____

_____

_____

_____

Have you made some efforts to simplify your life right now? If so, what have you done?

_____

_____

_____

_____

_____

_____

_____

_____

Have you been making daily to-do lists? If so, how is that working for you?

_____

_____

_____

_____

_____

_____

_____

Have you been able to say no and set limits where appropriate? Write about this below.

_____

_____

_____

_____

_____

_____

_____

_____

Have you been practicing patience and being gentle with yourself?

_____

_____

_____

_____

_____

_____

_____

As you explore the list of additional self-care guidelines for caring for your cognitive self, what other things have you been doing? (For example, taking time off work, bubble baths, breathing exercises, mini-vacations.)

_____

_____

_____

_____

_____

Nurturing Yourself: The Social Realm

How are you making an effort to stay connected to your family, friends, and community during this time?

_____

_____

_____

_____

_____

_____

Have your friendships changed during this time? If yes, explain. If not, write about why you think your friendships have not changed.

_____

_____

_____

_____

_____

_____

_____

Who are the selected family members you can turn to during this time? Name them and explain why you can turn to them.

_____

_____

_____

_____

_____

_____

_____

_____

Who are two people you can turn to anytime you need a friend? How have they been helpful to you?

_____

_____

_____

_____

_____

_____

_____

Have you reached out to a counselor or participated in a support group at this time? If so, describe what you have done.

_____

_____

_____

_____

_____

_____

Have you scheduled something that gives you pleasure each day? If so, what kind of things have you done?

_____

_____

_____

_____

_____

Have you done anything to brighten up your living space? If so, what have you done? If not, what could you plan to do?

_____

_____

_____

_____

_____

Nurturing Yourself: The Spiritual Realm

How do you nurture your spirit?

_____

_____

_____

_____

Do you express your faith/spirituality in a body of community? If so, describe what it is like for you and how it helps you.

_____

_____

_____

_____

_____

_____

_____

_____

Do you have a sacred space of sanctuary? If so, describe it. If not, is there any possibility you could create one? Where and how?

_____

_____

_____

_____

_____

_____

_____

_____

Do you pray? What do you pray for? Describe your prayer practices.

_____

_____

_____

_____

_____

_____

What do you feel gratitude for in your life right now?

_____

_____

_____

_____

_____

_____

_____

As you explore the list of additional self-care guidelines for caring for your spiritual self, what other things might you consider making use of? (For example, celebrate a sunrise, visit the great outdoors, find a spiritual director, sigh, create a divorce ceremony.)

_____

_____

_____

_____

_____

_____

_____

_____

_____

_____

_____

_____

_____

_____

Free Write

_____
_____
_____
_____
_____
_____
_____
_____
_____
_____
_____
_____
_____
_____
_____
_____
_____
_____
_____
_____
_____
_____
_____
_____
_____
_____

Touchstone Eight

Reach Out for Help

In the companion text...

We emphasized that the support and understanding of those around you is very important right now. You cannot make this journey alone. We also explored where you can turn for help and how to tell if you need professional help. Finding and working with a counselor was explored, as was participating in a divorce support group.

Are you able to reach out for help? If so, from whom? If not, why not?

_____

_____

_____

_____

_____

_____

_____

_____

_____

_____

_____

_____

Dr. Wolfelt's Rule of Thirds says that when you are in the wilderness of the divorce experience, you'll typically find that one-third of the people in your life will be neutral, one-third will be harmful and one-third will be truly supportive and helpful. Below, identify who is in your helpful one-third.

_____

_____

_____

_____

_____

_____

_____

_____

_____

_____

Who or what helps you feel hopeful?

_____

_____

_____

_____

_____

_____

_____

_____

_____

Who listens well as you tell your story?

_____

_____

_____

_____

_____

_____

Seeking Outside Help From a Counselor

Have you located a professional counselor as part of your support team? If so, describe your experience. If not, why haven't you felt the need or desire to try this out?

_____

_____

_____

_____

_____

_____

Spiritual Sources of Support and Counsel

Have you turned to any spiritual sources of support and counsel? If so, describe your experience. If not, why haven't you felt the need or desire to try this out?

_____

_____

_____

_____

_____

_____

_____

_____

_____

_____

How Do I Know if I Need Professional Help?

Review the "red flag" list of indications that suggest that professional assistance would be advisable (p. 166). Please note any of these criteria you meet. Then, write down the phone number of a place you can call to get a counseling appointment and make that call now.

_____

_____

_____

_____

_____

_____

_____

_____

_____

Support Groups

Have you looked into finding a support group? Are you in one now? What are your thoughts about and experiences with support groups?

_____

_____

_____

_____

_____

_____

_____

_____

_____

_____

Additional Resources

What additional resources related to seeking support have you made use of? (For example, books, newsletters, magazines, the internet.) What has this been like for you?

_____

_____

_____

_____

_____

_____

_____

_____

_____

_____

Free Write

_____
_____
_____
_____
_____
_____
_____
_____
_____
_____
_____
_____
_____
_____
_____
_____
_____
_____
_____
_____
_____
_____
_____
_____
_____
_____
_____
_____
_____

Touchstone Nine

Seek Integration, Not Resolution

In the companion text...

We defined what it means to integrate your divorce into your life instead of recovering from it or resolving it. We explored that with the experience of integration comes an ability to fully acknowledge the end of your marriage, feeling and acting like a single person with a future of your own design, a renewed sense of energy and confidence, and a capacity to become re-involved in the activities of life. We also reviewed a number of signs that integration is taking place in your journey. Finally, we explored the role of continued hope, trust, patience and faith in your achievement of integration.

In the space below, take the opportunity to write out where you see yourself in your own unique healing process. As you have learned about the concept of integration, what thoughts and feelings come to mind? Be compassionate with yourself if you are not as far along in this integration process as you (or others) would like. After all, through reading *Transcending Divorce* and completing this journal, you have certainly created some divine momentum in your healing.

_____

_____

_____

_____

_____

_____

_____

_____

Signs of Integration

Which, if any, of the listed signs of integration are you seeing in yourself right now? Note them below.

_____

_____

_____

_____

_____

_____

_____

_____

_____

_____

What reflections do you have from reading the sections titled
"Integration Means Living the Truth" and "Integration Means
Being Congruent"?

_____

_____

_____

_____

_____

_____

_____

_____

_____

_____

What reflections do you have from reading the section titled
"Integration Means Being Self-Responsible, Yet Patient"?

_____

_____

_____

_____

_____

_____

_____

_____

_____

_____

Do you have hope and trust that you will integrate your divorce into your life? What thoughts do you have related to the content of pages 177-178 , beginning with a section titled "Hope and Faith as Trust?"

_____

_____

_____

_____

_____

_____

_____

_____

_____

_____

_____

How are you choosing to make life good again?

_____

_____

_____

_____

_____

_____

_____

_____

_____

_____

_____

_____

Free Write

_____
_____
_____
_____
_____
_____
_____
_____
_____
_____
_____
_____
_____
_____
_____
_____
_____
_____
_____
_____
_____
_____
_____
_____
_____
_____
_____
_____

Touchstone Ten

Appreciate Your Transformation

In the companion text...

We affirmed that the journey through divorce is life-changing and that when you leave the wilderness of your divorce, you are simply not the same person you were when you entered your divorce wilderness. We also recognized that the transformation you see in yourself—and the personal growth you are experiencing as a consequence of the divorce—are not changes you would masochistically seek out. Still, we explored the various ways in which people often grow through divorce. We also reviewed some of the additional signs that you have integrated your divorce transition into your life.

How are you discovering that you are being transformed by your divorce experience?

_____

_____

_____

_____

_____

_____

_____

_____

_____

_____

_____

_____

What changes have you seen in yourself (new attitudes, insights, skills) during this time in your life?

_____

_____

_____

_____

_____

_____

_____

_____

_____

_____

_____

_____

Various definitions of growth were provided in the book. Explore your own experiences with these definitions about growth in the space provided below.

Growth Means More Meaning and Purpose

_____

_____

_____

_____

_____

_____

_____

Growth Means More Energy and Life Force

_____

_____

_____

_____

_____

_____

_____

Growth Means More Feelings

_____

_____

_____

_____

_____

_____

_____

_____

_____

Growth Means More Love, Intimacy and Connection

_____

_____

_____

_____

_____

_____

_____

_____

_____

Growth Means More Possibilities

_____

_____

_____

_____

_____

_____

_____

_____

Growth Means More Quality of Experience

_____

_____

_____

_____

_____

_____

_____

_____

Growth Means More Satisfaction and Fulfillment

_____

_____

_____

_____

_____

_____

_____

_____

_____

Growth Means More Truth

_____

_____

_____

_____

_____

_____

_____

_____

Growth Means More Faith and Spirituality

_____

_____

_____

_____

_____

_____

_____

Growth Means Transcendence

_____

_____

_____

_____

_____

_____

_____

_____

_____

Carrying Your Transformation Forward

What can you do to continue to carry your transformation forward?

_____

_____

_____

_____

_____

_____

_____

_____

_____

_____

_____

_____

_____

_____

_____

Free Write

_____

_____

_____

_____

_____

_____

_____

_____

_____

_____

_____

_____

_____

_____

_____

_____

_____

_____

_____

_____

_____

_____

_____

_____

_____

_____

Continuing Your Journey

In the months and years to come, I invite you to revisit this journal and reflect on the ongoing and ever-changing nature of your divorce experience. How has your life changed? In what ways have you developed new perspectives on your divorce? Please take a few minutes from time to time and write down updates in the blank pages that follow.

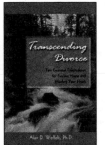

Transcending Divorce

Ten Essential Touchstones for Finding Hope and Healing Your Heart

After years of being encouraged to contribute a book on divorce loss, Dr. Wolfelt has responded with this compassionate new guide. When it comes to grief and loss, divorce is one of the most heartbreaking for many people.

With empathy and wisdom, Dr. Wolfelt walks the reader through ten essential Touchstones for hope and healing. Readers are encouraged to give attention to the need to mourn your lost relationship before "moving on" to a new relationship.

If you're hurting after a divorce, this book is for you. Warm, direct and easy to understand, this is a book you will not want to put down.

ISBN 978-1-879651-50-0 • 128 pages • softcover • $14.95

ALSO BY ALAN WOLFELT

The Transcending Divorce Support Group Guide

Guidance and Meeting Plans for Facilitators

When we are experiencing feelings of grief and loss during and after a divorce, we need the support and compassion of our fellow human beings. Divorce support groups provide an opportunity for this healing kind of support.

This book is for those who want to facilitate an effective divorce group. It includes 12 meeting plans that interface with Dr. Wolfelt's *Transcending Divorce* book and its companion journal. Each week, group members read a portion of *Transcending Divorce* and write down their thoughts and feelings in the guided journal. Using the *Support Group Guide* in conjunction with the other two texts, support group leaders can simply and effectively combine divorce grief education with compassionate support—all in a practical, 12-meeting structure.

ISBN 978-1-879651-56-2 • 44 pages • softcover • $12.95